MAD LIBS®
DIARY OF A WIMPY KID
MAD LIBS

by Patrick Kinney

Mad Libs
An Imprint of Penguin Random House

MAD LIBS
Penguin Young Readers Group
An Imprint of Penguin Random House LLC

Published by Mad Libs,
an imprint of Penguin Random House LLC,
345 Hudson Street, New York, New York 10014.
Printed in the USA.

ISBN 9780843183535
9 10 8

In case you have forgotten what adjectives, adverbs, nouns, and verbs are, here is a quick review:

An ADJECTIVE describes something or somebody. *Lumpy, soft, ugly, messy,* and *short* are adjectives.

An ADVERB tells how something is done. It modifies a verb and usually ends in "ly." *Modestly, stupidly, greedily,* and *carefully* are adverbs.

A NOUN is the name of a person, place, or thing. *Sidewalk, umbrella, bridle, bathtub,* and *nose* are nouns.

A VERB is an action word. *Run, pitch, jump,* and *swim* are verbs. Put the verbs in past tense if the directions say PAST TENSE. *Ran, pitched, jumped,* and *swam* are verbs in the past tense.

When we ask for A PLACE, we mean any sort of place: a country or city (*Spain, Cleveland*) or a room (*bathroom, kitchen*).

An EXCLAMATION or SILLY WORD is any sort of funny sound, gasp, grunt, or outcry, like *Wow!, Ouch!, Whomp!, Ick!,* and *Gadzooks!*

When we ask for specific words, like a NUMBER, a COLOR, an ANIMAL, or a PART OF THE BODY, we mean a word that is one of those things, like *seven, blue, horse,* or *head.*

When we ask for a PLURAL, it means more than one. For example, *cat* pluralized is *cats.*

MAD LIBS® is fun to play with friends, but you can also play it by yourself! To begin with, DO NOT look at the story on the page below. Fill in the blanks on this page with the words called for. Then, using the words you have selected, fill in the blank spaces in the story.

Now you've created your own hilarious MAD LIBS® game!

FAMILY TIME

NOUN _____

ADJECTIVE _____

PLURAL NOUN _____

ADJECTIVE _____

PLURAL NOUN _____

PART OF THE BODY (PLURAL) _____

ADJECTIVE _____

VERB ENDING IN "ING" _____

ANIMAL _____

VERB ENDING IN "ING" _____

NOUN _____

VERB ENDING IN "ING" _____

NOUN _____

ADJECTIVE _____

MAD LIBS

FAMILY TIME

Being stuck at home during a/an _____-storm is the
NOUN

WORST! My _____ brother Rodrick has been banging on
ADJECTIVE

his _____ all day. It's driving me totally _____,
PLURAL NOUN   ADJECTIVE

and I'm not the only one! Dad has _____ stuffed in his
PLURAL NOUN

_____, and my _____ brother Manny
PART OF THE BODY (PLURAL)   ADJECTIVE

won't stop _____. Even our _____, Sweetie,
VERB ENDING IN "ING"   ANIMAL

is upset by all the noise. For a while he was just _____
VERB ENDING IN "ING"

in the corner, but then he peed on the _____! Well, someone
NOUN

else can clean it up because I'm not doing it! Mom is the only one who

doesn't mind Rodrick's music. She's been _____ around
VERB ENDING IN "ING"

the house and tried to get *me* to join her. When I said there was no

way, she told me not to be such a wet _____— whatever
NOUN

that means. All I can say is that I'll be really _____ if school
ADJECTIVE

is canceled tomorrow!

MAD LIBS® is fun to play with friends, but you can also play it by yourself! To begin with, DO NOT look at the story on the page below. Fill in the blanks on this page with the words called for. Then, using the words you have selected, fill in the blank spaces in the story.

Now you've created your own hilarious MAD LIBS® game!

RODRICK'S SCHOOL REPORT

NUMBER _____

PART OF THE BODY _____

A PLACE _____

NOUN _____

OCCUPATION _____

NOUN _____

VERB ENDING IN "ING" _____

NOUN _____

LAST NAME _____

PLURAL NOUN _____

LAST NAME _____

OCCUPATION _____

NOUN _____

ADJECTIVE _____

OCCUPATION _____

PART OF THE BODY _____

MAD LIBS®

RODRICK'S SCHOOL REPORT

Everyone knows George Washington invented the _____-
NUMBER

dollar bill because it has his _____ on it, but I bet you
PART OF THE BODY

don't know anything else about the guy. He was born in (the)

_____, and when he was a kid, he chopped down his father's
A PLACE

favorite tree with a/an _____. After that, he became a/an
NOUN

_____ and fought against the French in India. That's why
OCCUPATION

it was called the French and Indian _____. When he was
NOUN

done _____, he married a/an _____ named
VERB ENDING IN "ING" NOUN

Martha _____. I guess she loved him, even though he had
LAST NAME

teeth made of _____. They lived on a farm called Mount
PLURAL NOUN

_____until George got tired of being a/an _____
LAST NAME OCCUPATION

and decided to help the United States win its _____ from
NOUN

England. Everyone thought George was so _____, they
ADJECTIVE

made him the country's first _____. When he died, George
OCCUPATION

was buried inside a mountain called Mount Rushmore because it

already had his _____ on it.
PART OF THE BODY

MAD LIBS® is fun to play with friends, but you can also play it by yourself! To begin with, DO NOT look at the story on the page below. Fill in the blanks on this page with the words called for. Then, using the words you have selected, fill in the blank spaces in the story.

Now you've created your own hilarious MAD LIBS® game!

WANTED AD

NOUN _____

NOUN _____

PLURAL NOUN _____

ADJECTIVE _____

A PLACE _____

NOUN _____

PART OF THE BODY _____

NOUN _____

PLURAL NOUN _____

ADJECTIVE _____

COLOR _____

ARTICLE OF CLOTHING _____

NUMBER _____

A PLACE _____

PLURAL NOUN _____

MAD LIBS®

WANTED AD

_____PLAYER WANTED
NOUN

Tired of being a/an _____? Sick of not having any
NOUN

_____ want to go out with you? Well, today's ur
PLURAL NOUN

_____ day, cuz you just might be the newest member of
ADJECTIVE

Löded Diper. What we want:

- Someone who can practice every night at (the) _____.
A PLACE

- Someone who can learn all our hits, like "_____
NOUN

Overlode" and "Exploded _____."
PART OF THE BODY

- Someone with a/an _____ we can use for our world tour this
NOUN

summer. Even better if it's got _____ painted on the sides.
PLURAL NOUN

- Someone who looks _____. Bonus points for
ADJECTIVE

_____ hair or a black leather _____.
COLOR   ARTICLE OF CLOTHING

So, if ur serious about joining the # _____ band in the world,
NUMBER

prove you have what it takes. Open auditions are this Saturday at

Rodrick's house. (If we're not there, look for us in (the) _____
A PLACE

parking lot wear we'll probly be putting fake _____ on people's
PLURAL NOUN

cars.)

MAD LIBS® is fun to play with friends, but you can also play it by yourself! To begin with, DO NOT look at the story on the page below. Fill in the blanks on this page with the words called for. Then, using the words you have selected, fill in the blank spaces in the story.

Now you've created your own hilarious MAD LIBS® game!

AN EMAIL FROM MANNY'S TEACHER

ADJECTIVE _____

SILLY WORD _____

ARTICLE OF CLOTHING _____

TYPE OF FOOD (PLURAL) _____

NOUN _____

FIRST NAME (FEMALE) _____

NOUN _____

LAST NAME _____

ANIMAL _____

ADJECTIVE _____

VERB _____

LAST NAME _____

VERB _____

MAD LIBS
AN EMAIL FROM MANNY'S TEACHER

Dear Mr. and Mrs. Heffley,

Unfortunately, Manny had a/an ＿＿＿＿＿＿ day at preschool today.
                                     ADJECTIVE

When I greeted him as he arrived, he said, "Hi, Ms. ＿＿＿＿＿＿."
                                                       SILLY WORD

Then, when I helped him take off his ＿＿＿＿＿＿＿＿, he said my
                                   ARTICLE OF CLOTHING

breath smelled like ＿＿＿＿＿＿＿. I thought his ＿＿＿＿＿＿
                 TYPE OF FOOD (PLURAL)   NOUN

would improve after he got settled, but he then threw an art project

that ＿＿＿＿＿＿ had been working on in the ＿＿＿＿＿＿.
     FIRST NAME (FEMALE)   NOUN

I brought the group together to sing "Old ＿＿＿＿＿＿," hoping
                                        LAST NAME

this would help Manny get back on track. But when the children

started to sing "with an oink-oink here," Manny made ＿＿＿＿＿＿
                                               ANIMAL

noises instead. Manny is usually such a/an ＿＿＿＿＿＿ child.
                                            ADJECTIVE

Perhaps you can ＿＿＿＿＿＿ with him about his behavior today.
                      VERB

                          Regards,

                            Ms. ＿＿＿＿＿＿
                                       LAST NAME

PS: I haven't seen Rodrick since I taught him years ago. Did he

ever learn to ＿＿＿＿＿＿ his name?
                    VERB

MAD LIBS® is fun to play with friends, but you can also play it by yourself! To begin with, DO NOT look at the story on the page below. Fill in the blanks on this page with the words called for. Then, using the words you have selected, fill in the blank spaces in the story.

Now you've created your own hilarious MAD LIBS® game!

ROWLEY'S DIARY

ADJECTIVE _____

A PLACE _____

FIRST NAME (MALE) _____

SILLY WORD _____

NOUN _____

ADJECTIVE _____

NOUN _____

TYPE OF FOOD _____

COLOR _____

VERB ENDING IN "ING" _____

ADJECTIVE _____

TYPE OF FOOD _____

PLURAL NOUN _____

ADJECTIVE _____

VERB _____

ADJECTIVE _____

MAD LIBS

ROWLEY'S DIARY

Dear Diary,

Today me and Mommy had a/an _______________ day together, and it
ADJECTIVE
was so much fun! First, she took me to (the) _______________ and bought
A PLACE
me a new Dinoblazer action figure named Terrordactyl, but I didn't
like that scary name, so I named him _______________. Then, we went
FIRST NAME (MALE)
and saw a funny movie. I think it was called *Willy* _______________.
SILLY WORD
It was about a man who lived in a big _______________, and he had
NOUN
so much candy that he thought it would be _______________ to give
ADJECTIVE
it all to a/an _______________ named Charlie. Charlie was nice but
NOUN
Veruca _______________ was mean, and so was this other girl named
TYPE OF FOOD
_______________ who was always _______________ gum. Mommy
COLOR — VERB ENDING IN "ING"
said I was such a/an _______________ boy that she would take me to
ADJECTIVE
get _______________. I covered it in whipped cream and chocolate
TYPE OF FOOD
_______________, and when I ate it, my tummy was _______________.
PLURAL NOUN — ADJECTIVE
Then we went home and played "I _______________ You Because" with
VERB
Daddy. Today was the most _______________ day ever.
ADJECTIVE

MAD LIBS® is fun to play with friends, but you can also play it by yourself! To begin with, DO NOT look at the story on the page below. Fill in the blanks on this page with the words called for. Then, using the words you have selected, fill in the blank spaces in the story.

Now you've created your own hilarious MAD LIBS® game!

GREG'S THANK-YOU NOTE

FIRST NAME (FEMALE) _____

ADJECTIVE _____

ADJECTIVE _____

NOUN _____

SAME NOUN _____

NOUN _____

FIRST NAME (MALE) _____

VERB ENDING IN "ING" _____

VERB _____

SAME FIRST NAME (MALE) _____

ADJECTIVE _____

ADVERB _____

NOUN _____

MAD LIBS

GREG'S THANK-YOU NOTE

Dear Aunt _____,
          FIRST NAME (FEMALE)

Thank you so much for the awesome gift! It was the most

_____ birthday present ever. All my friends will be so
ADJECTIVE

_____ that I have my own _____. I love the way
ADJECTIVE   NOUN

the _____ looks on my _____! I'm sorry Uncle
    SAME NOUN   NOUN

_____ was sick and couldn't come to the party. Mom said
FIRST NAME (MALE)

he was _____ all night. It must have been hard for you
       VERB ENDING IN "ING"

to _____ with all that noise! Was the present from both of
   VERB

you, or did Uncle _____ get me something else? If he
                  SAME FIRST NAME (MALE)

did, can he bring it to me when he's feeling _____? Or better
                                             ADJECTIVE

yet, you can bring it over _____. Thank you again, and to
                          ADVERB

make things easy for you, I'd like a/an _____ for my next
                                        NOUN

birthday.

Love,

Greg

MAD LIBS® is fun to play with friends, but you can also play it by yourself! To begin with, DO NOT look at the story on the page below. Fill in the blanks on this page with the words called for. Then, using the words you have selected, fill in the blank spaces in the story.

Now you've created your own hilarious MAD LIBS® game!

PARENTING ADVICE COLUMN

NOUN _____

PLURAL NOUN _____

ADJECTIVE _____

NOUN _____

NOUN _____

PLURAL NOUN _____

VERB ENDING IN "ING" _____

ADVERB _____

NOUN _____

ADJECTIVE _____

NOUN _____

NOUN _____

NOUN _____

MAD☺LIBS
PARENTING
ADVICE COLUMN

"Your Son and Puberty: One Mother's Advice"

by Susan Heffley

When a/an _____ begins to experience the _____
                NOUN   PLURAL NOUN

that come with adolescence, the transformation can be uncomfortable,

awkward, or even _____. But given the right guidance, a/an
                      ADJECTIVE

_____ can learn to welcome, and even celebrate, the transition
      NOUN

into _____-hood. One of my _____, who I won't
         NOUN   PLURAL NOUN

identify by name, is now _____ this period in his life.
                         VERB ENDING IN "ING"

I _____ noticed that he had horrible _____ odor,
      ADVERB   NOUN

but I was _____ not to say anything. Instead, I simply put
              ADJECTIVE

a stick of _____ on his bed with a note attached that said,
               NOUN

"Your _____ will always love you, no matter what you smell
          NOUN

like." By giving him the _____ he needs, I'm sure Greg will
                             NOUN

be able to solve this problem on his own.

MAD LIBS® is fun to play with friends, but you can also play it by yourself! To begin with, DO NOT look at the story on the page below. Fill in the blanks on this page with the words called for. Then, using the words you have selected, fill in the blank spaces in the story.

Now you've created your own hilarious MAD LIBS® game!

GREG AND ROWLEY'S LAWN SERVICE

ADJECTIVE _____

PART OF THE BODY (PLURAL) _____

NOUN _____

VERB _____

NOUN _____

VERB _____

CELEBRITY (MALE) _____

CELEBRITY (FEMALE) _____

NOUN _____

VERB _____

VERB _____

ADVERB _____

NUMBER _____

ANIMAL _____

PLURAL NOUN _____

MAD LIBS®
GREG AND ROWLEY'S
LAWN SERVICE

Nothing is more _____ than the appearance of your lawn.
                      ADJECTIVE

So why would you put it in the _____ of just anyone?
                                PART OF THE BODY (PLURAL)

Give your lawn the _____ it deserves by hiring VIP Lawn Service!
                        NOUN

No matter what you _____, we'll do it all! We can:
                          VERB

• Mow your _____*
                NOUN

• _____ your leaves**
      VERB

Celebrities like _____ and _____ pamper
                  CELEBRITY (MALE)   CELEBRITY (FEMALE)

themselves, so why shouldn't you?! With our _____-winning
                                              NOUN

service, you'll _____ like a VIP, too. So don't wait!
                    VERB

_____ us today at 555-2941, and we'll _____
      VERB   ADVERB

schedule an appointment!

*We will not mow within _____ feet of _____ poop.
                          NUMBER   ANIMAL

**The cost is five _____ per leaf.
                    PLURAL NOUN

MAD LIBS® is fun to play with friends, but you can also play it by yourself! To begin with, DO NOT look at the story on the page below. Fill in the blanks on this page with the words called for. Then, using the words you have selected, fill in the blank spaces in the story.

Now you've created your own hilarious MAD LIBS® game!

LÖDED DIPER RIDER

PLURAL NOUN _____

ADJECTIVE _____

TYPE OF FOOD _____

TYPE OF LIQUID _____

ANIMAL (PLURAL) _____

PART OF THE BODY _____

NOUN _____

NOUN _____

NOUN _____

FIRST NAME (MALE) _____

ADJECTIVE _____

NOUN _____

ADJECTIVE _____

ADJECTIVE _____

ANIMAL _____

SAME ANIMAL _____

TYPE OF FOOD _____

ANIMAL (PLURAL) _____

MAD LIBS

LÖDED DIPER RIDER

Famous rock bands often have a list of _____ they want in
PLURAL NOUN

their backstage dressing room. Löded Diper isn't _____, but
ADJECTIVE

that didn't stop them from making a list of their own!

- Five _____ pizzas
  TYPE OF FOOD

- Ten bottles of _____
  TYPE OF LIQUID

- Three bags of gummy _____
  ANIMAL (PLURAL)

- Three boxes of _____-breakers
  PART OF THE BODY

- A sixty-five-inch plasma _____
  NOUN

- A video-game console with *Call of* _____, *Grand Theft*
  NOUN

  _____, and *Super* _____ *Brothers*
  NOUN   _FIRST NAME (MALE)_

- DVDs of *The* _____ *Knight Returns,* _____
  ADJECTIVE   _NOUN_

  Wars, and _____ *and Dumber*
  ADJECTIVE

- One extra-_____ hot tub
  ADJECTIVE

- One _____
  ANIMAL

- Food for the _____ (either _____ or some
  SAME ANIMAL   _TYPE OF FOOD_

  _____)
  ANIMAL (PLURAL)

MAD LIBS® is fun to play with friends, but you can also play it by yourself! To begin with, DO NOT look at the story on the page below. Fill in the blanks on this page with the words called for. Then, using the words you have selected, fill in the blank spaces in the story.

Now you've created your own hilarious MAD LIBS® game!

GREG'S SUMMER VACATION

ADJECTIVE _____

TYPE OF FOOD (PLURAL) _____

PLURAL NOUN _____

FIRST NAME (FEMALE) _____

NOUN _____

ADJECTIVE _____

PLURAL NOUN _____

VERB ENDING IN "ING" _____

OCCUPATION _____

VERB _____

PART OF THE BODY (PLURAL) _____

TYPE OF LIQUID _____

PERSON IN ROOM (MALE) _____

NOUN _____

"How I Spent My Summer Vacation"

by Greg Heffley

As usual, my summer was pretty _____. I *wanted* to eat

ADJECTIVE

_____ and play video _____ for three

TYPE OF FOOD (PLURAL)   PLURAL NOUN

months, but _____ wouldn't allow it. She said I needed

FIRST NAME (FEMALE)

to be outside, where I could get some fresh _____, like

NOUN

a/an "_____" kid. So I ended up at the pool most days.

ADJECTIVE

It was always jam-packed with _____, so I didn't do

PLURAL NOUN

much _____. But I did spend a lot of time with the

VERB ENDING IN "ING"

_____, Heather Hills. We really understood each other

OCCUPATION

without having to _____ a thing. Like, if she snapped her

VERB

_____, I knew she wanted me to get her a bottle of

PART OF THE BODY (PLURAL)

_____. But when _____ barfed near the

TYPE OF LIQUID   PERSON IN ROOM (MALE)

snack bar and Heather looked at me to clean it up, I realized that

summer isn't a good time to start a serious _____.

NOUN

MAD LIBS® is fun to play with friends, but you can also play it by yourself! To begin with, DO NOT look at the story on the page below. Fill in the blanks on this page with the words called for. Then, using the words you have selected, fill in the blank spaces in the story.

Now you've created your own hilarious MAD LIBS® game!

GREG SEES THE FUTURE (PART ONE)

NOUN _____

NUMBER _____

FIRST NAME _____

OCCUPATION _____

NUMBER _____

NOUN _____

A PLACE _____

COLOR _____

VEHICLE _____

SILLY WORD _____

ANIMAL _____

CELEBRITY _____

PERSON IN ROOM _____

SILLY WORD _____

PART OF THE BODY _____

NOUN _____

PLURAL NOUN _____

MAD LIBS
GREG SEES THE FUTURE
(PART ONE)

Looking deep into his crystal _____, Greg predicts what the
                              NOUN
future will bring you. Here's what you can expect!

You will:

- have at least _____ children. They will all be named
                    NUMBER

  _____.
   FIRST NAME

- be a/an _____ and make _____ dollars a year.
              OCCUPATION   NUMBER

- live in a/an _____ in (the) _____.
                    NOUN   A PLACE

- drive a/an _____ _____. Your license plate will
                  COLOR   VEHICLE

  say "_____."
         SILLY WORD

- own a pet _____ named _____.
                 ANIMAL   CELEBRITY

- be best friends with _____.
                        PERSON IN ROOM

- get a tattoo that says "_____" on your _____.
                            SILLY WORD   PART OF THE BODY

- win a/an _____ by guessing how many _____
                NOUN   PLURAL NOUN

  are in a jar.

Even though you now know your future, still try to look surprised

when it all comes true!

MAD LIBS® is fun to play with friends, but you can also play it by yourself! To begin with, DO NOT look at the story on the page below. Fill in the blanks on this page with the words called for. Then, using the words you have selected, fill in the blank spaces in the story.

Now you've created your own hilarious MAD LIBS® game!

TIME CAPSULE LETTER

VERB ENDING IN "ING" _____

NOUN _____

PLURAL NOUN _____

PLURAL NOUN _____

TYPE OF FOOD _____

ANIMAL _____

OCCUPATION (PLURAL) _____

VERB _____

NOUN _____

PLURAL NOUN _____

NOUN _____

OCCUPATION _____

CELEBRITY _____

VERB _____

PLURAL NOUN _____

MAD LIBS®

TIME CAPSULE LETTER

Dear people of the future,

If you are _____ this, then you have found the time
       VERB ENDING IN "ING"

capsule buried by me, Greg Heffley (and my _____ Rowley).
                           NOUN

When I was alive, most people lived in _____ and drove
                               PLURAL NOUN

_____ to get from one place to another. We ate many types
PLURAL NOUN

of food, like _____ and _____. Many adults went
        TYPE OF FOOD   _ANIMAL_

to work, and the ones who were _____ were the best paid.
                         OCCUPATION (PLURAL)

For fun, kids liked to play games like hide-and- _____ or
                                     VERB

capture the _____, but most kids would rather have been
          NOUN

inside playing video _____. The main _____
                  PLURAL NOUN   _NOUN_

in charge of our country was called the _____. Right now
                               OCCUPATION

our leader is someone called _____. If time travel has been
                        CELEBRITY

invented, please go back in time and _____ me with a
                               VERB

million _____. (Don't worry about Rowley.)
       PLURAL NOUN

                                 Signed,

                                 Greg Heffley

MAD LIBS® is fun to play with friends, but you can also play it by yourself! To begin with, DO NOT look at the story on the page below. Fill in the blanks on this page with the words called for. Then, using the words you have selected, fill in the blank spaces in the story.

Now you've created your own hilarious MAD LIBS® game!

THE SCHOOL DANCE

CELEBRITY _____

A PLACE _____

ADJECTIVE _____

PLURAL NOUN _____

PART OF THE BODY _____

VERB ENDING IN "ING" _____

LAST NAME _____

NOUN _____

VERB _____

PLURAL NOUN _____

NOUN _____

VERB ENDING IN "ING" _____

OCCUPATION (PLURAL) _____

OCCUPATION _____

COLOR _____

ANIMAL _____

ADJECTIVE _____

NOUN _____

MAD LIBS®

THE SCHOOL DANCE

"School Dance Is Alarming"

by Holly Hills

Last Saturday, _____ Middle School held its first dance of
                      CELEBRITY

the year. The theme was "Midnight in (the) _____," even
                                            A PLACE

though it started at 3:00 p.m. The event got off to a/an _____
                                                          ADJECTIVE

start, with only the _____ dancing at first. The boys, on the
                      PLURAL NOUN

other _____, were all _____ on the bleachers.
       PART OF THE BODY   VERB ENDING IN "ING"

Then, Principal _____ grabbed the _____ and
                  LAST NAME   NOUN

said over the loudspeakers that anyone who didn't _____
                                                   VERB

would have to clean _____ from the soccer _____
                     PLURAL NOUN   NOUN

the following weekend. That got everyone _____, even
                                          VERB ENDING IN "ING"

some of the _____. Mr. Phillips and _____
             OCCUPATION (PLURAL)   OCCUPATION

Powell danced to the new _____ _____ song.
                          COLOR   ANIMAL

They looked really _____, so most of us were relieved
                    ADJECTIVE

when someone pulled the _____ alarm and the dance
                         NOUN

ended. Overall, it seemed like some people had an okay time.

MAD LIBS® is fun to play with friends, but you can also play it by yourself! To begin with, DO NOT look at the story on the page below. Fill in the blanks on this page with the words called for. Then, using the words you have selected, fill in the blank spaces in the story.

Now you've created your own hilarious MAD LIBS® game!

GREG SEES THE FUTURE (PART TWO)

COLOR _____

ARTICLE OF CLOTHING (PLURAL) _____

ARTICLE OF CLOTHING (PLURAL) _____

PART OF THE BODY (PLURAL) _____

TYPE OF FOOD (PLURAL) _____

TYPE OF LIQUID _____

PLURAL NOUN _____

VERB _____

SILLY WORD _____

PLURAL NOUN _____

PLURAL NOUN _____

A PLACE _____

ANIMAL (PLURAL) _____

VERB _____

PLURAL NOUN _____

PERSON IN ROOM _____

MAD LIBS®
GREG SEES THE FUTURE
(PART TWO)

In the future:

- everyone will dress the same. For our futuristic uniform, we'll all wear _____ _____ and
  <u>COLOR</u> <u>ARTICLE OF CLOTHING (PLURAL)</u>
  _____ on our heads.
  <u>ARTICLE OF CLOTHING (PLURAL)</u>

- anytime we clap our _____, robots will serve us
  <u>PART OF THE BODY (PLURAL)</u>
  _____ and glasses of _____.
  <u>TYPE OF FOOD (PLURAL)</u> <u>TYPE OF LIQUID</u>

- it will be illegal for _____ to _____ on a Sunday.
  <u>PLURAL NOUN</u> <u>VERB</u>

- instead of saying, "Hello," we'll all say "_____."
  <u>SILLY WORD</u>

- aliens will visit our planet and bring us _____.
  <u>PLURAL NOUN</u>

- people won't go to the gym anymore. Instead, they'll lift
  _____ in (the) _____.
  <u>PLURAL NOUN</u> <u>A PLACE</u>

- a person's wealth will be measured by how many _____
  <u>ANIMAL (PLURAL)</u>
  he or she owns.

- people won't drive cars anymore, because they'll _____
  <u>VERB</u>
  around on _____ instead.
  <u>PLURAL NOUN</u>

- _____ will be president of the United States!
  <u>PERSON IN ROOM</u>

MAD LIBS® is fun to play with friends, but you can also play it by yourself! To begin with, DO NOT look at the story on the page below. Fill in the blanks on this page with the words called for. Then, using the words you have selected, fill in the blank spaces in the story.

Now you've created your own hilarious MAD LIBS® game!

LETTER TO GRANDPA, FROM SUSAN

VERB ENDING IN "ING" _____

A PLACE _____

ADJECTIVE _____

PLURAL NOUN _____

ANIMAL _____

VERB _____

NOUN _____

TYPE OF LIQUID _____

VERB _____

FIRST NAME (FEMALE) _____

NOUN _____

NOUN _____

NOUN _____

MAD☺LIBS®
LETTER TO GRANDPA, FROM SUSAN

Thank you for _____ Greg and Rodrick while Frank
<small>VERB ENDING IN "ING"</small>

and I spend the week in (the) _____. To make things
<small>A PLACE</small>

_____ for you, I'm including a list of dos and don'ts.
<small>ADJECTIVE</small>

Do remind the boys to brush their _____ every night.
<small>PLURAL NOUN</small>

Don't allow Greg to walk through the house if he's stepped in

_____ poop.
<small>ANIMAL</small>

Do make sure the boys _____ up in the morning. You may
<small>VERB</small>

need to bang the _____ lids together.
<small>NOUN</small>

Don't let Rodrick drink straight from the _____ carton.
<small>TYPE OF LIQUID</small>

Do make sure the boys _____ for twenty minutes each night.
<small>VERB</small>

_____'s *Web* for Greg and a/an _____ magazine
<small>FIRST NAME (FEMALE)</small>   <small>NOUN</small>

for Rodrick.

Have a great week with the boys. I'm sure they'll be happy to spend some

time with their grandpa. Love, Susan

PS: If they give you too much _____, put Santa's _____
<small>NOUN</small>   <small>NOUN</small>

above the fireplace. They won't misbehave as long as he's around!

MAD LIBS® is fun to play with friends, but you can also play it by yourself! To begin with, DO NOT look at the story on the page below. Fill in the blanks on this page with the words called for. Then, using the words you have selected, fill in the blank spaces in the story.

Now you've created your own hilarious MAD LIBS® game!

GREG SENDS A VALENTINE

FIRST NAME (FEMALE) _____

NOUN _____

PART OF THE BODY _____

ADVERB _____

PLURAL NOUN _____

ADVERB _____

PLURAL NOUN _____

VERB _____

NOUN _____

NOUN _____

NOUN _____

VERB ENDING IN "S" _____

NOUN _____

NOUN _____

NOUN _____

FIRST NAME (FEMALE) _____

MAD LIBS®

GREG SENDS A VALENTINE

Beloved _____,
FIRST NAME (FEMALE)

For you, a/an _____ blazes in my _____
NOUN   PART OF THE BODY

So _____ that the embers alone could
ADVERB

bring a thousand _____ to a boil,
PLURAL NOUN

So _____ that it causes _____
ADVERB   PLURAL NOUN

everywhere to despair.

Let the bonfire of my love

_____ you in its _____.
VERB   NOUN

Only your _____ could quench the _____
NOUN   NOUN

that _____ me.
VERB ENDING IN "S"

To you, I pledge my _____, my _____,
NOUN   NOUN

my _____.
NOUN

—Greg

PS: If you're not interested, could you scratch your name out and

give this to _____?
FIRST NAME (FEMALE)

MAD LIBS® is fun to play with friends, but you can also play it by yourself! To begin with, DO NOT look at the story on the page below. Fill in the blanks on this page with the words called for. Then, using the words you have selected, fill in the blank spaces in the story.

Now you've created your own hilarious MAD LIBS® game!

THE HEFFLEY FAMILY CHRISTMAS CARD

PLURAL NOUN _____

VERB _____

ADJECTIVE _____

ADJECTIVE _____

VERB ENDING IN "ING" _____

PLURAL NOUN _____

NOUN _____

VERB ENDING IN "ING" _____

ADJECTIVE _____

PLURAL NOUN _____

VERB _____

ARTICLE OF CLOTHING (PLURAL) _____

PLURAL NOUN _____

TYPE OF FOOD (PLURAL) _____

ARTICLE OF CLOTHING (PLURAL) _____

MAD LIBS
THE HEFFLEY FAMILY
CHRISTMAS CARD

Dear family and _____,
<u>PLURAL NOUN</u>

It's hard to _____, but the end of another year is upon
<u>VERB</u>

us. I'm _____ to say that the Heffleys are doing quite
<u>ADJECTIVE</u>

well. Frank is as _____ as ever at work but enjoys
<u>ADJECTIVE</u>

_____ with his model _____ during his free
<u>VERB ENDING IN "ING"</u>   <u>PLURAL NOUN</u>

time. As for myself, I'm still writing my column, "Susan Says," for the

local _____. The boys are _____ so much!
<u>NOUN</u>   <u>VERB ENDING IN "ING"</u>

Manny uses his _____ potty regularly now. Only rarely
<u>ADJECTIVE</u>

do we find _____ behind the couch. Greg and Rodrick
<u>PLURAL NOUN</u>

continue to _____ as well. Every week, it seems, Greg is
<u>VERB</u>

fitting into another pair of Rodrick's old _____.
<u>ARTICLE OF CLOTHING (PLURAL)</u>

Is anyone making any New Year's _____? I've decided to eat
<u>PLURAL NOUN</u>

less _____ and exercise more. I guess I'd better break
<u>TYPE OF FOOD (PLURAL)</u>

out the _____! Best wishes in the coming year!
<u>ARTICLE OF CLOTHING (PLURAL)</u>

Love,

The Heffleys

MAD LIBS® is fun to play with friends, but you can also play it by yourself! To begin with, DO NOT look at the story on the page below. Fill in the blanks on this page with the words called for. Then, using the words you have selected, fill in the blank spaces in the story.

Now you've created your own hilarious MAD LIBS® game!

ROWLEY'S BIRTHDAY INVITATION

NOUN _____

ADJECTIVE _____

NUMBER _____

ADJECTIVE _____

PLURAL NOUN _____

VERB ENDING IN "ING" _____

ADJECTIVE _____

PLURAL NOUN _____

ANIMAL _____

COLOR _____

A PLACE _____

PLURAL NOUN _____

NOUN _____

TYPE OF FOOD _____

TYPE OF LIQUID _____

PLURAL NOUN _____

PLURAL NOUN _____

NOUN _____

MAD LIBS®
ROWLEY'S BIRTHDAY INVITATION

You're invited to a birthday _____ for a very _____
                              NOUN   ADJECTIVE

boy!

Join us this Saturday to celebrate Rowley turning _____
                                                   NUMBER

years old. It was a/an _____ hit when we all dressed as
                        ADJECTIVE

_____ last year, but Rowley is _____ up
PLURAL NOUN   VERB ENDING IN "ING"

and says he'd like a superhero party, since he's "a/an _____
                                                        ADJECTIVE

kid now." Please though, no bad _____ like Doctor
                                 PLURAL NOUN

_____ or the _____ Goblin. We'll all meet at
ANIMAL   COLOR

(the) _____ at 2:00 p.m., where the _____ will
      A PLACE   PLURAL NOUN

play laser _____ before enjoying some _____
            NOUN   TYPE OF FOOD

and grape _____—Rowley's favorites. Rowley has more
           TYPE OF LIQUID

_____ than he can play with, but if you decide to bring
PLURAL NOUN

a present, he's really into coloring _____ these days. Our
                                      PLURAL NOUN

_____ is getting so big!
NOUN

MAD LIBS® is fun to play with friends, but you can also play it by yourself! To begin with, DO NOT look at the story on the page below. Fill in the blanks on this page with the words called for. Then, using the words you have selected, fill in the blank spaces in the story.

Now you've created your own hilarious MAD LIBS® game!

REVERSE BUCKET LIST

TYPE OF LIQUID _____

ANIMAL _____

NOUN _____

FIRST NAME _____

PART OF THE BODY _____

NUMBER _____

VERB ENDING IN "ING" _____

ANIMAL _____

PART OF THE BODY _____

A PLACE _____

PART OF THE BODY _____

TYPE OF FOOD _____

A PLACE _____

TYPE OF FOOD _____

FIRST NAME _____

ARTICLE OF CLOTHING _____

A PLACE _____

MAD☉LIBS®

REVERSE BUCKET LIST

"Things I Never Want to Do Again"

by Greg Heffley

- Eat cereal with _____ instead of milk
  TYPE OF LIQUID

- Test to see if a/an _____ is ticklish
  ANIMAL

- Sleep in the same _____ as _____
  NOUN   FIRST NAME

- Rub suntan lotion on Grandpa's _____
  PART OF THE BODY

- Go more than _____ days without _____
  NUMBER   VERB ENDING IN "ING"

- Go camping without bringing _____ repellant
  ANIMAL

- Ride the _____ Shaker
  PART OF THE BODY

- Spend a week with Rowley's family at (the) _____
  A PLACE

- Slam my _____ in the car door
  PART OF THE BODY

- Clean _____ from Manny's plastic potty
  TYPE OF FOOD

- Go to (the) _____ after sitting in _____
  A PLACE   TYPE OF FOOD

- Trust _____ when they tell me it's "Silly
  FIRST NAME
  _____ Day" at (the) _____
  ARTICLE OF CLOTHING   A PLACE

MAD LIBS® is fun to play with friends, but you can also play it by yourself! To begin with, DO NOT look at the story on the page below. Fill in the blanks on this page with the words called for. Then, using the words you have selected, fill in the blank spaces in the story.

Now you've created your own hilarious MAD LIBS® game!

VIDEO GAME COMPETITION ADVERTISEMENT

NOUN _____

A PLACE _____

PLURAL NOUN _____

PART OF THE BODY _____

ADJECTIVE _____

PERSON IN ROOM _____

PLURAL NOUN _____

VERB _____

VERB ENDING IN "ING" _____

PLURAL NOUN _____

PLURAL NOUN _____

NUMBER _____

A PLACE _____

ARTICLE OF CLOTHING (PLURAL) _____

ADJECTIVE _____

VERB _____

NOUN _____

PLURAL NOUN _____

MAD LIBS®
VIDEO GAME COMPETITION
ADVERTISEMENT

Call yourself a/an _____? Then come to (the) _____
$\qquad$ NOUN $\qquad$ A PLACE

and prove it this Saturday in the Twisted Wizard Tournament!

Show off your _____ by going toe-to-_____
$\qquad$ PLURAL NOUN $\qquad$ PART OF THE BODY

with some of the most _____ Twisted Wizard players in
$\qquad$ ADJECTIVE

the area. All the legends will be there including five-time champion,

_____. Why just slay _____ and _____
PERSON IN ROOM $\qquad$ PLURAL NOUN $\qquad$ VERB

orcs in your basement when you can be _____ to win
$\qquad$ VERB ENDING IN "ING"

_____, prizes, and your own place among the Twisted
PLURAL NOUN

Wizard _____?!
$\qquad$ PLURAL NOUN

First place will win a/an _____-dollar gift certificate to (the)
$\qquad$ NUMBER

_____. Second- and third-place contestants will win Twisted
A PLACE

Wizard _____, courtesy of _____
$\qquad$ ARTICLE OF CLOTHING (PLURAL) $\qquad$ ADJECTIVE

Topic. And there's more! The first fifty players to _____ will
$\qquad$ VERB

get a free can of Mountain _____. So walk, run, or get your
$\qquad$ NOUN

_____ to drive you. Just be there!
PLURAL NOUN

MAD LIBS® is fun to play with friends, but you can also play it by yourself! To begin with, DO NOT look at the story on the page below. Fill in the blanks on this page with the words called for. Then, using the words you have selected, fill in the blank spaces in the story.

Now you've created your own hilarious MAD LIBS® game!

GREG'S DIARY ENTRY
ABOUT SANTA'S SCOUT

ADJECTIVE _____

VERB _____

PLURAL NOUN _____

LAST NAME _____

VERB ENDING IN "ING" _____

ARTICLE OF CLOTHING (PLURAL) _____

VERB ENDING IN "ING" _____

NOUN _____

VERB _____

ADJECTIVE _____

VERB _____

NOUN _____

NOUN _____

FIRST NAME (MALE) _____

VERB _____

ANIMAL (PLURAL) _____

MAD LIBS®
GREG'S DIARY ENTRY
ABOUT SANTA'S SCOUT

The holidays make me a/an _____ wreck. I know that
<small>ADJECTIVE</small>

every time I _____ up, it just means less _____
<small>VERB</small> <small>PLURAL NOUN</small>

on Christmas morning. And knowing that Santa _____
<small>LAST NAME</small>

can always see me, even when I'm _____, really creeps
<small>VERB ENDING IN "ING"</small>

me out! Lately I've been wearing _____ to bed,
<small>ARTICLE OF CLOTHING (PLURAL)</small>

because I don't need him _____ me in my underwear.
<small>VERB ENDING IN "ING"</small>

And now that Mom brought out this old _____ called
<small>NOUN</small>

"Santa's Scout," things are even WORSE. Supposedly, it's his job to

watch how kids _____ and then report back to Saint Nick
<small>VERB</small>

at the _____ Pole. So I try not to _____ anywhere
<small>ADJECTIVE</small> <small>VERB</small>

near him, but it's hard to tell where he'll show up. Just this morning, I

went in the bathroom to take a/an _____ and he was perched
<small>NOUN</small>

on the _____! Even though I think _____ was
<small>NOUN</small> <small>FIRST NAME (MALE)</small>

the one who put him there, I won't be able to _____ until
<small>VERB</small>

the holidays are over. And if this doll *is* real, I hope he gets trampled by

one of Santa's _____ the next time he's up north.
<small>ANIMAL (PLURAL)</small>

Download on the
App Store

GET IT ON
Google Play

Download Mad Libs today!

Join the millions of Mad Libs fans
creating wacky and wonderful
stories on our apps!